THE *Phoenix* JOURNAL

52 WEEKS OF REFLECTION AND ASPIRATIONAL ACTIVITIES

— C. L. Jordan —

Feisty Scholar Publications

www.feistyscholar.com

Cover designed by Mibl Art.

THE Phoenix JOURNAL

978-1-913619-18-3 (paperback)

978-1-913619-19-0 (eBook)

For news and details of upcoming publications from this author, visit:

www.cherjones.co.uk

THE
Phoenix
JOURNAL

If you've bought this book, you are probably looking for guidance on how to fine-tune your thinking and achieve your goals. Congratulations on taking that first step towards the life you want.

The Phoenix Journal provides a comprehensive set of 52 aspirational tasks. Every week, a new task will guide and inform your thoughts. You will explore your current unhelpful patterns, reflect on how these habits were formed, and consider how you can make positive changes.

In between, journaling pages allow you to chronicle your efforts and feelings. Your journal pages are sprinkled with motivational quotes, affirmations for you to use or space to create your own, plus 'Top Tips' and 'Remember' points to help you on your journey. For those of you aiming to build relationships, there are also 'Making Connections' conversation starters.

Together these activities will guide you toward achieving your goals. Because you have a choice: stagnate in your current position or rise like the phoenix into the life you desire.

WEEK 1: TAKING STOCK

No matter how ambitious you are, there are only so many hours in a day. Before you can make changes, it is crucial to take stock of your current commitments. Fill in the timetable below with your current schedule. Then colour code each one as either a 'need to do' or 'want to do'.

Sun	Mon	Tue	Wed	Thu	Fri	Sat

Now consider these questions whilst completing your journaling pages:

Which activities make you happy?
What could be the advantages and disadvantages of making changes?
What would you add to your schedule if you had more time?
Do you have a good balance between work and rest?

JOURNAL

> **A winner is a dreamer who never gives up.**
>
> Nelson Mandela

Date:

....
....
....
....
....
....
....
....
....

Date:

....
....
....
....
....
....
....
....

Date:

....
....
....
....
....
....
....
....

Affirmation

A unique quality I have is my ability to learn and adapt.

A unique quality I have is ...

Date:

....

....

....

....

....

....

Date:

....

....

....

....

....

Phoenix
JOURNAL

Making Connections

If you could download a quality or skill straight into your brain, what would you choose and why?

Date:

Date:

....

....

....

....

....

....

....

....

....

....

....

....

....

....

....

....

....

....

....

....

....

....

WEEK 2: FROM LITTLE SEEDS...

Think back to eleven-year-old you. It was then that you were planting the seeds for your current reality. Perhaps you watered those seeds daily and they grew to be all you imagined. But if not, it might help you to find purpose by revisiting these ambitions. Consider the following questions:

What were your passions?

How did you imagine your life to be at the age you are now?

Are any of these points now irrelevant or outdated?

Are they still dreams that you would one day like to pursue?

If not, are there aspects of them that still interest you?

What advice would you give your younger self?

JOURNAL

Date:

....

....

....

....

....

....

....

....

....

....

> 66
>
> You have brains in your head. You
> have feet in your shoes. You can
> steer yourself in any direction you
> choose.
>
> Doctor Seuss
> 99

Date:

....

....

....

....

....

....

....

....

Date:

....

....

....

....

....

....

....

....

Phoenix
JOURNAL

Remember

When going through hell, keep on going—wise words from Churchill. Keep placing one foot in front of the other. This philosophy is bound to take you further than running in circles or freezing in fear.

Date:

Date:

JOURNAL

TOP TIP

Stack habits you want to create along with other tasks. For example, packing your gym bag at the same time as you pick out your clothes for the next day. Or making overnight oats for breakfast at the same time as preparing dinner.

Date:

....
....
....
....
....
....
....
....
....
....
....
....

Date:

....
....
....
....
....
....
....
....
....
....
....
....

WEEK 3: GROWTH MINDSET

Researchers such as Carol Dweck describe two types of mindset: fixed and growth. Those with a fixed mindset might struggle to progress and find themselves wracked with anxiety. They see their abilities as permanent, so if they fail, they deem themselves incapable. People with growth mindsets see themselves as able to change. They do not baulk when facing challenges and see failure as useful learning experiences.

Look at the criteria below. Which do you feel apply to you? Could any of these characteristics hold you back? What behaviours could you change to move from fixed to growth?

FIXED

Resents or fears feedback

Feels threatened by others' success

Views effort as pointless

Gives up easily

Is wary of challenges

Wants to look smart

GROWTH

Feels inspired by the success of others

Learns from criticism

Views effort as the path to mastery

Is resilient in the face of setbacks

Embraces challenges

Desires to learn

JOURNAL

> ❝
> The tragedy of life doesn't lie in not reaching your goals. The tragedy lies in having no goals to reach.
>
> Benjamin E. Mays
> ❞

Date:

....
....
....
....
....
....
....
....
....

Date:

....
....
....
....
....
....
....
....

Date:

....
....
....
....
....
....
....
....

Phoenix
JOURNAL

Making Connections

What was your childhood nickname? Did you like it? If you didn't, what would you have chosen for yourself?

Date:

Date:

Affirmation

I embrace my mistakes because they are essential learning experiences.

I embrace...

Date:

....
....
....
....
....
....

Date:

....
....
....
....
....
....

WEEK 4: FEATHERS FOR FLIGHT

You want to be the phoenix, soaring towards your goal. But sometimes you may feel weighed down by insecurities and anxiety. One way to conquer this is to counter such negative thoughts with positive memories. These could include a time you:

- helped somebody
- received recognition for something you did well
- earned an award
- accomplished something
- faced a fear
- stuck up for yourself

Write a positive memory under each feather. You don't have to fill them all in now; you can always return and add to them later as you make more memories.

JOURNAL

> **"**
> There is nothing noble in being superior to your fellow man; true nobility is being noble to your former self.
>
> Ernest Hemingway
> **"**

Date:

....

....

....

....

....

....

....

....

....

Date:

....

....

....

....

....

....

....

Date:

....

....

....

....

....

....

....

JOURNAL

Remember

Forgiving yourself is just as important, if not more so, than forgiving others. How can you prove what a good person you are if you keep telling yourself you are a bad one?

Date:

Date:

Phoenix
JOURNAL

TOP TIP

Create a list of goals. Some people call it a bucket list, but I find that a little morbid! This can help you prioritise what you want.

Date:

Date:

WEEK 5: YOUR REFLECTION

In the mirror outline below, sketch yourself. Don't worry, nobody is expecting you to be an artist!

Now think carefully about your personality traits. In one colour, list the characteristics that will help you achieve your goal. For example: organised, determined and proactive. In a different colour, list characteristics that could become potential obstacles. For example: highly strung, tardy, and stubborn. Being aware of how the person looking back at you in the mirror could help or hinder you is an important step towards achieving your goals.

Phoenix JOURNAL

Date:

....

....

....

....

....

....

....

....

....

....

> "
> Success often comes to those who dare to act. It seldom goes to the timid who are ever afraid of the consequences.
>
> Jawaharlal Nehru
> "

Date:

....

....

....

....

....

....

....

....

....

....

Date:

....

....

....

....

....

....

....

....

....

....

Remember

People get themselves lost in mazes for fun. The challenge is to find your way out. If you knew the route, it would be a pointless exercise. Just like life, the joy is in the exploration.

Date: | Date:

Phoenix
JOURNAL

Making Connections

What is your idea of a perfect day trip?

Date:

Date:

WEEK 6: TAKE IT OR LEAVE IT?

Change is a journey. The choices that you make now will affect whether you reach your destination or not. You can choose to keep your current behaviors – pack them – or leave them behind you. Only you can decide how helpful they are to achieving your goal.

Look at the behaviors you wrote around your picture in the last activity. Which will help you, and which will hold you back? Write the ones you want to keep within the outline of the suitcase and the ones you want to leave behind outside it.

JOURNAL

Date:

....

....

....

....

....

....

....

....

....

....

> Motivation is what gets you started. Habit is what keeps you going.
>
> Jim Ryun

Date:

....

....

....

....

....

....

....

....

Date:

....

....

....

....

....

....

....

....

Affirmation

I am grateful for good friends in my life.

I am grateful for...

Date:

....

....

....

....

....

....

Date:

....

....

....

....

....

....

Remember

They are called growing pains for a reason. When life flows smoothly, there is no reason to change. It is by facing adversity that we are forced to grow.

Date: _____   Date: _____

....

....

....

....

....

....

....

....

....

....

....

WEEK 7: BANISH THE SHADOWS

Like shadows, negative self-talk can mirror our every move. We are often our own worst critics. That voice, whispering (or perhaps hollering) from the shadows of our minds, telling us that we are unworthy, a disappointment, stupid. But as with most things that terrify us, the power that negative thoughts have over us exists because they go unchallenged. If we drag them from the shadows and examine them, we might find that they aren't as intimidating as we first believe. List examples of negative self-talk that you've experienced. Now look for evidence to discredit this thought.

NEGATIVE THOUGHT	CONTRADICTORY EVIDENCE

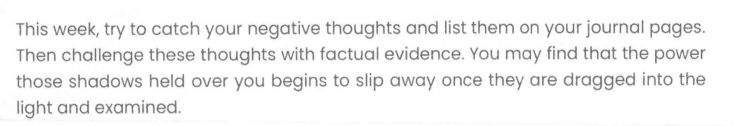

This week, try to catch your negative thoughts and list them on your journal pages. Then challenge these thoughts with factual evidence. You may find that the power those shadows held over you begins to slip away once they are dragged into the light and examined.

Phoenix
JOURNAL

Date:

....

....

....

....

....

....

....

....

....

> "
> Two roads diverged in a wood and I
> - I took the one less travelled by,
> and that has made all the
> difference.
>
> Robert Frost
> "

Date:

....

....

....

....

....

....

....

Date:

....

....

....

....

....

....

....

Phoenix
JOURNAL

Making Connections

If you won the lottery, how would you spend it?

Date:

Date:

Phoenix JOURNAL

Date:

....

....

....

....

....

....

....

....

....

....

....

Date:

....

....

....

....

....

....

....

....

....

....

....

WEEK 8: PAST VICTORIES

List three past victories. How did you overcome the obstacles you faced?

Perhaps you got yourself out of debt by transferring credit card balances to interest-free lenders. Or you sought the guidance of a mentor to get an assignment in on time. The possibilities are as individual as you are.

JOURNAL

Date:

....
....
....
....
....
....
....
....
....

> 66
>
> I can't change the direction of the wind, but I can adjust my sails so I always reach my destination.
>
> Jimmy Dean
>
> 99

Date:

....
....
....
....
....
....
....
....

Date:

....
....
....
....
....
....
....
....

Phoenix JOURNAL

Date:

Date:

Affirmation

I am positive that my upcoming interview will lead to a job offer.

I am positive...

Date:

....

....

....

....

....

....

Date:

....

....

....

....

....

....

WEEK 9: DIAMOND 9

When deciding on goals, it is helpful to clarify your priorities. Look at the list. At the top of the diamond, put the item that motivates you the most. At the bottom, place the least important thing to you. The rest go in the remaining spaces. There are more items on the list than spaces, so you will have to pick. Feel free to substitute any of your preferred items for those on the list. When setting your goals in future weeks, it will be helpful to look back at this diagram to see if they align with your priorities.

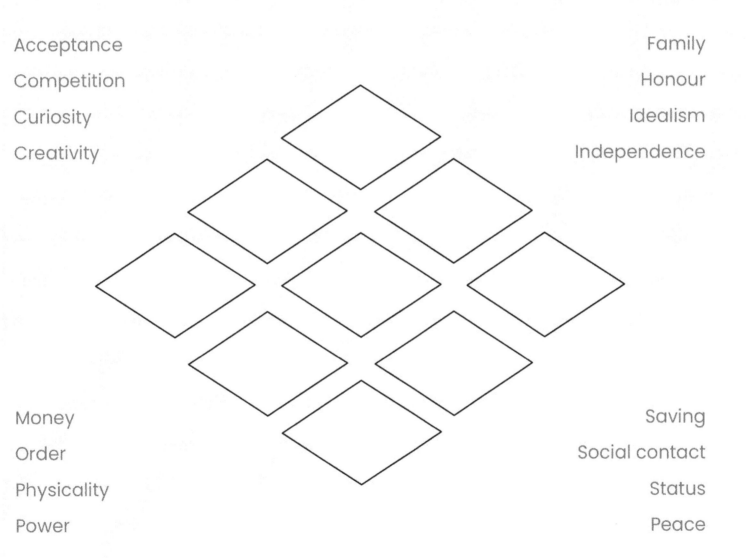

Acceptance

Competition

Curiosity

Creativity

Family

Honour

Idealism

Independence

Money

Order

Physicality

Power

Saving

Social contact

Status

Peace

JOURNAL

> **"**
> If you don't like something, change it; if you can't change it, change your attitude.
>
> Maya Angelou
> **"**

Date:

....
....
....
....
....
....
....
....
....
....

Date:

....
....
....
....
....
....
....
....
....

Date:

....
....
....
....
....
....
....
....
....

Phoenix
JOURNAL

Making Connections

What was something unusual about your childhood?

Date:

Date:

Phoenix
JOURNAL

TOP TIP

A great way of visualising the future that you want is to create a vision board. It is simply a place to display pictures, words and other sources that show your goal. The idea is to look at it regularly to manifest its contents.

Date:

....
....
....
....
....
....
....
....
....
....
....

Date:

....
....
....
....
....
....
....
....
....
....
....

WEEK 10: YOUR IDEAL SELF

Knowing what you want is the first step to achieving it. If your goals include self-development, considering the following questions may give you some insight.

What kind of person do you aspire to be?

Can you name somebody who embodies these qualities already?

Which qualities make them so appealing?

What personal traits are important to you?

Do you seek people with these traits for friendships/ romantic relationships? Why?

What do you think other people might say about you at the moment?

What would you like them to say about you?

What changes will you need to make to instigate this?

Phoenix
JOURNAL

> "
>
> We can not solve our problems with the same thinking we used when we created them.
>
> Albert Einstein
>
> "

Date:

....
....
....
....
....
....
....
....
....

Date:

....
....
....
....
....
....
....
....

Date:

....
....
....
....
....
....
....
....

Phoenix
JOURNAL

Remember

Nothing is stronger than hope.

Date:

....
....
....
....
....
....
....
....
....
....
....
....

Date:

....
....
....
....
....
....
....
....
....
....
....
....

Affirmation

This week I am prioritising my health by attending three gym classes.

This .... I am.............................

Date:

....

....

....

....

....

....

Date:

....

....

....

....

....

WEEK 11: CROSSROADS 1

You are standing at a crossroads with paths leading off in four directions. The signposts read 'head', 'heart', 'household' and 'humanity'. There are aspects of each that tempt you to choose that path. If you are lucky, they will lead you towards the same destination. If not, you may feel torn about which to choose. Recognising the influences pulling you in each direction can help to clarify your thinking and manage your anxiety. Over the next four weeks, we will reflect on these directions, starting with 'head'.

What is your head telling you to do?

....

....

....

Would it affect anything in your life negatively?

....

....

What could the implications of following your dream be?

....

....

What benefits would meeting your goal bring to your life?

....

....

How about the lives of those around you?

....

....

JOURNAL

> 66
>
> I have been bent and broken, but - I hope - into a better shape.
>
> Charles Dickens
>
> 99

Date:

....
....
....
....
....
....
....
....
....

Date:

....
....
....
....
....
....
....

Date:

....
....
....
....
....
....
....

Phoenix
JOURNAL

Making Connections

If you had a crystal ball that could tell you
your future, would you want to know?

Date:

Date:

Affirmation

I am kind to myself and others.

I am kind ...

Date:

....

....

....

....

....

....

....

Date:

....

....

....

....

....

....

....

WEEK 12: CROSSROADS 2

What is your heart telling you to do?

....

....

....

....

....

Head

Heart

Household

Humanity

Is your heart pulling you in a
different direction from your head?

....

....

....

What is the same/different about
what it's telling you?

....

....

....

What would you choose to do if
you could not fail?

....

....

....

What would a younger, unjaded
you want you to do?

....

....

....

JOURNAL

> 66
>
> I have not failed 10,000 times. I have succeeded in proving that those 10,000 ways will not work.
>
> Thomas Edison
>
> 99

Date:

....

....

....

....

....

....

....

....

Date:

....

....

....

....

....

....

....

....

Date:

....

....

....

....

....

....

....

Phoenix JOURNAL

TOP TIP

If you want to break a bad habit, create friction when performing it. For example, put that cookie jar on the top shelf, take your credit card out of your wallet or set a screen time setting on your phone!

Date:

Date:

Phoenix JOURNAL

Remember

Your mind is like a house, and the windows are the eyes you are looking out through. If they need cleaning, you may see the world as dark and dismal. If they are blown, the outside world may appear perpetually rainy. This is worth bearing in mind before you pass judgement on the outside world.

Date: _____

Date: _____

....

....

....

....

....

....

....

....

....

....

....

WEEK 13: CROSSROADS 3

Your household is the people under your roof, plus anybody in your extended friends and family network for whom you feel responsible.

What are the expectations and hopes that the people in your household have for you?

....
....
....
....

Head
Heart
Household
Humanity

What would the people in your household tell you to do?

....
....
....

Will your decision affect them adversely?

....
....
....

Could they benefit in the long or short term?

....
....

What practical aspects will you need to consider (e.g. financial)?

....
....

JOURNAL

> 66
>
> Ambition is the path to success.
> Persistence is the vehicle you
> arrive in.
>
> Bill Bradley
>
> 99

Date:

....

....

....

....

....

....

....

....

....

....

Date:

....

....

....

....

....

....

....

....

Date:

....

....

....

....

....

....

....

....

Affirmation

I am a careful manager of my finances which means my finances are steadily improving.

I am a careful manager of...

Date:

....

....

....

....

....

....

Date:

....

....

....

....

....

....

Phoenix JOURNAL

Making Connections

What areas of your life do you hope will have changed a year from now? How?

Date: _____

Date: _____

....
....
....
....
....
....
....
....
....
....

WEEK 14: CROSSROADS 4

Humanity is anybody else your decision could affect, such as peers, colleagues, and society as a whole.

Will your decision influence anybody in your wider circle?

....

....

....

....

Head

Heart

Household

Humanity

How might your decision benefit others?

Could it disadvantage anybody?

....

....

....

JOURNAL

> "
> No one can make you feel inferior without your consent.
>
> Eleanor Roosevelt
> "

Date:

....
....
....
....
....
....
....
....
....
....

Date:

....
....
....
....
....
....
....
....

Date:

....
....
....
....
....
....
....
....

Phoenix
JOURNAL

Remember

Extrinsic events are often neither good nor bad. It is our perception that gives it weight either way. Try not to think of yourself as being at the mercy of a world you can't control, but instead directing a mind that you can.

Date:

Date:

TOP TIP

Try to save a little money every week. Start small if you like but create the habit. Your future self will thank you for it.

Date:

....

....

....

....

....

....

....

....

....

....

....

Date:

....

....

....

....

....

....

....

....

....

....

WEEK 15: FRIEND OR FOE?

To move forward, it's important to be honest with yourself. Do your current behaviours make you a friend or a foe in your journey towards success? Too often we are our own worst enemies and become stuck with habits and behaviours that hold us back. Look at the statements below. Circle the extent to which you agree or disagree with them (one meaning 'disagree completely' and five meaning 'agree completely').

	1	2	3	4	5
When I want to achieve something, I make a plan.					
I get demoralised when I am met with an obstacle.					
I always meet my deadlines.					
People consider me a reliable person.					
I do the bare minimum required.					
If I fail at a task, I reflect and adapt my method.					
I use the same methods even if they've failed in the past.					
I consider the way I learn best and adapt my techniques to fit my strengths.					
I get annoyed or anxious when given feedback.					
I seek advice from more knowledgeable others.					

Which area will you try to improve and how?	

Phoenix
JOURNAL

Date:

....
....
....
....
....
....
....
....
....

> "
> I attribute my success to this - I never gave or took an excuse.
>
> Florence Nightingale
> "

Date:

....
....
....
....
....
....
....
....
....

Date:

....
....
....
....
....
....
....
....
....

Affirmation

A dream I will achieve this month is to
see a musical in a West End theatre.

A dream I will achieve this .... is to ...

Date:

....

....

....

....

....

....

Date:

....

....

....

....

....

....

Phoenix
JOURNAL

Making Connections

Did you have a childhood friend that greatly
impacted your life? How?

Date:

....

....

....

....

....

....

....

....

....

....

Date:

....

....

....

....

....

....

....

....

....

....

WEEK 16: WHEEL OF LIFE

On a scale from 1 to 6 (with 6 being the ideal), how satisfied are you with each area of your life? Colour in the relevant number of sections. This will help you pinpoint the areas where you need to put in the most effort. It is good to get into the habit of reviewing your satisfaction levels, so this activity will be repeated later in the journal.

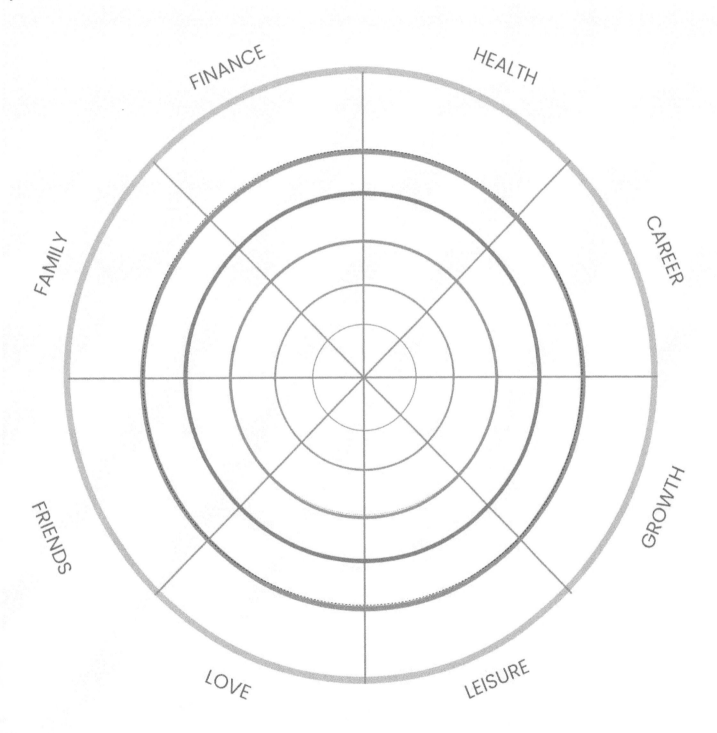

JOURNAL

Date:

....
....
....
....
....
....
....
....
....

> "
> The best way to predict the future is to create it.
>
> Abraham Lincoln
> "

Date:

....
....
....
....
....
....
....
....
....

Date:

....
....
....
....
....
....
....
....
....

Phoenix JOURNAL

Date:

....

....

....

....

....

....

....

....

....

....

....

Date:

....

....

....

....

....

....

....

....

....

....

....

JOURNAL

TOP TIP

Turn all of the hangers in your closet the other way around. Each time you wear a piece, put it back the correct way. Set a deadline. If there are still hangers facing the wrong way when you reach it, donate those items to charity.

Date:

Date:

WEEK 17: SWOT ANALYSIS

Before deciding on a strategy to reach your goals, it is helpful to look at your existing strengths and weaknesses. This will allow you to anticipate any help or resources you might require. In addition, considering opportunities and threats will mean you can build them into your plan.

STRENGTHS

S

WEAKNESSES

W

OPPORTUNITIES

O

THREATS

T

Phoenix
JOURNAL

> It's never too late to be what you might have been.
>
> George Eliot

Date:

Date:

Affirmation

I am free of destructive doubt and fear.

I am free of...

Date:

....
....
....
....
....
....
....

Date:

....
....
....
....
....
....
....

Phoenix
JOURNAL

Making Connections

What was your favourite childhood memory?

Date: _____

....
....
....
....
....
....
....
....
....
....
....

Date: _____

....
....
....
....
....
....
....
....
....
....
....

WEEK 18: SMART GOALS

Setting effective targets takes practice. However, it is well worth learning how to do so as it can mean the difference between success and failure. First of all, your goal should be specific. For example: I will complete a half marathon. It should also be measurable, in this case, 13.1 miles and perhaps a time limit. There is no point in setting unachievable goals. So if you have never run in a race before, you might want to set your sights a little lower. Make sure your goal is relevant to you. Generic goals won't be as effective. Lastly, your goal should be time bound. Hazy deadlines lead to poor outcomes. In this case, entering a race on a set date will give you something to work towards. You may wish to review this activity when setting yourself goals at various points on your journey.

SPECIFIC	
MEASURABLE	
ACHIEVABLE	
RELEVANT	
TIME BOUND	

JOURNAL

Date:

....
....
....
....
....
....
....
....
....

> "
> The way you talk to yourself creates your reality.
>
> Unknown author
> "

Date:

....
....
....
....
....
....
....
....

Date:

....
....
....
....
....
....
....
....

Phoenix
JOURNAL

Making Connections

What is a goal you have in life?

Date:

Date:

....

....

....

....

....

....

....

....

....

....

....

....

....

....

....

....

....

....

....

....

Remember

You deserve to be loved.

Date:	Date:

....
....

....
....

....
....

....
....

....
....

....
....

....
....

....
....

....
....

....
....

....
....

WEEK 19: THREE SMALL STEPS

The journey towards success can be broken down into small footsteps. Looking at the end destination and the distance you have to travel can be overwhelming. But if you chunk the journey up into the next three footsteps you need to take, it will feel far more manageable. In the box below, write the goal you want to achieve. Then below it, write the three steps you will take to begin the journey towards it. Of course, you might change and refine your goal on the way. Use your journaling pages to repeat this activity as often as you like, but it will be replicated in The Phoenix Journal twice more to remind you to review your goals and footsteps.

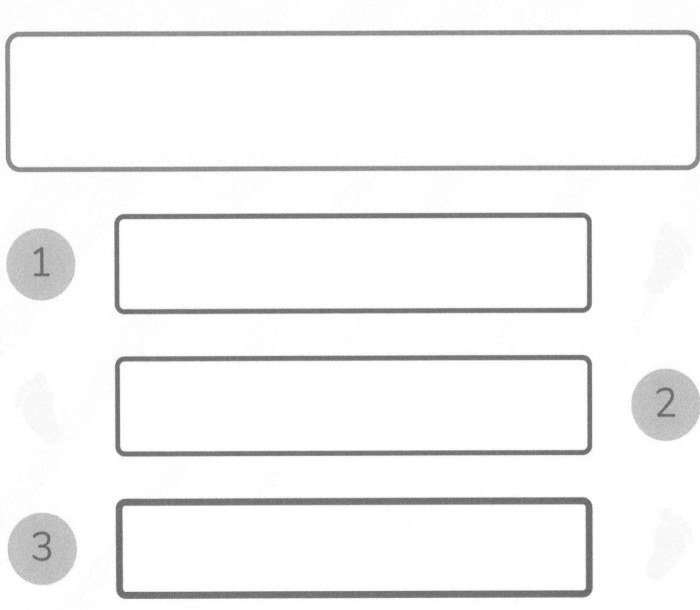

JOURNAL

Date:

....
....
....
....
....
....
....
....
....

> " Success is not final. Failure is not fatal. It is the courage to continue that counts.
>
> Winston Churchill "

Date:

....
....
....
....
....
....
....
....

Date:

....
....
....
....
....
....
....
....

JOURNAL

TOP TIP

Ask yourself 'why' more often. It will help you evaluate everything in your life from habits to relationships. Once you have the answer you can decide whether to scrap it or not.

Date:

....

....

....

....

....

....

....

....

....

....

....

Date:

....

....

....

....

....

....

....

....

....

....

....

Affirmation

I believe in myself and each day I take
the necessary steps to reach my goals.

I believe...

Date:

Date:

WEEK 20: PLOTTING THE JOURNEY

It is all very well being asked to plot the first three steps towards your goal. But what about all the ones that come after? If you aren't sure where you will go next, you need to do some research. Start with the questions below and then use your journal pages this week to add anything else you think of.

What questions do you have?

Where could you find the answers?

Which sites could you read up on?

Who can you ask?

How will you contact them?

Are there any deadlines you need to take note of?

JOURNAL

Date:

> "
> Sometimes the only available transportation is a leap of faith.
>
> Margaret Sheppard
> "

Date:

Date:

Phoenix JOURNAL

Making Connections

What values are most important to you?
Why?

Date: _____

Date: _____

....

....

....

....

....

....

....

....

....

....

....

....

....

....

....

....

....

....

....

....

Phoenix
JOURNAL

Remember

This too will pass. Like the changing of the seasons or a cloud passing across the sun, very little in life is permanent.

Date:

....
....
....
....
....
....
....
....
....
....
....

Date:

....
....
....
....
....
....
....
....
....
....
....

WEEK 21: VISUALISING SUCCESS

How will you know that you have been successful? It might seem obvious to you, but don't let yourself fall into the trap of fuzzy goals. Perhaps you want to be a writer. There, that's your goal. But when do you stamp it as achieved? When you write your first short story, finish a manuscript, get a book deal? It is better to set clear parameters for success. That way, you can reward yourself for your achievement and set a new goal. Use the prompts below to help you clarify your goals.

1. My goal is …

   Example: My goal is to publish my first short story.

2. I will know I've been successful because…

   Example: I will know I've been successful because I will be published in a Christmas special of X magazine.

3. My goal will be completed by…

   Example: My goal will be completed by the end of July because editors will be buying stories for Christmas editions at this time.

JOURNAL

> " Do one thing every day that scares you.
>
> Eleanor Roosevelt "

Date:

....

....

....

....

....

....

....

....

Date:

....

....

....

....

....

....

....

Date:

....

....

....

....

....

....

....

Affirmation

I forgive myself so that I am free to be happy.

I forgive...

Date:

....
....
....
....
....
....

Date:

....
....
....
....
....
....

Phoenix JOURNAL

Making Connections

What unique quality or skill do you have?

Date: _____

Date: _____

....
....
....
....
....
....
....
....
....
....
....

WEEK 22: SELF-SABOTAGE

You could be sabotaging your success. Too much time on social media, constantly checking your phone, eating extra snacks when dieting: these are all examples of self-sabotage. Whilst journaling this week, reflect on times that you have sabotaged yourself. List some examples below and then consider how you might avoid doing so in the future.

SELF-SABOTAGE	AVOIDED BY...

JOURNAL

Date:

> "
> If it doesn't challenge you, it won't change you.
>
> Unknown author
> "

Date:

Date:

Phoenix JOURNAL

TOP TIP

Use the 5 x 5 rule. Will this matter in five years? If not, then don't spend more than five minutes worrying about it.

Date:

Date:

Phoenix JOURNAL

Remember

The most efficient way to climb a mountain is to make a plan. The same logic goes for tackling problems. You can't conquer a challenge you pretend doesn't exist.

Date:

Date:

WEEK 23: SILVER LINING

We have already considered the positives we could take from the challenges we face. You might call this the silver lining. Use the prompt questions below to revisit this idea. Then, look for the positives in difficult situations whilst journaling this week.

Have your priorities changed due to the obstacle you faced?

....

....

Do you have more insight into certain people or professions?

....

....

Were there any personal skills you had to learn, practise or revise?

....

....

Have you gained any insights that you could share in the form of advice?

....

....

Have you developed a greater understanding of how to assert yourself in a particular situation?

....

....

What would you change about how you handled it if you faced a similar obstacle?

....

....

Phoenix JOURNAL

> A comfort zone is a beautiful place,
> but nothing ever grows there.
>
> Unknown author

Date:

....
....
....
....
....
....
....
....
....

Date:

....
....
....
....
....
....
....
....

Date:

....
....
....
....
....
....
....
....

Affirmation

I am free from the temptation to emotionally eat because I find comfort in my friendships and taking time for self-care.

I am free from...

Date:

....

....

....

....

....

....

Date:

....

....

....

....

....

....

Phoenix
JOURNAL

Making Connections

What motivates you? Does that change in different areas of your life?

Date:

....
....
....
....
....
....
....
....
....
....
....

Date:

....
....
....
....
....
....
....
....
....
....
....

WEEK 24: MANIFEST

Some schools of thought suggest it is possible to manifest your dreams into reality. In the spaces below, sketch out something you desire. If you aren't a fan of drawing, you may wish to paste in a magazine cutting instead.

JOURNAL

> How you love yourself is how you
> teach others to love you.
>
> Rupi Kaur

Date:

Date:

Date:

Phoenix
JOURNAL

Making Connections

If you were an animal, what kind would you be and why?

Date:

Date:

Remember

You can only do your best.

Date:

Date:

WEEK 25: IF/THEN

An excellent way to prepare for and overcome obstacles and self-sabotage is to use if/then sentences. Think about the possible scenario and decide on a 'then' to overcome it. This will relieve the pressure when you're put on the spot!

For example: If I am invited to the beach on a morning I should be revising, then I will agree to meet my friends there later and use the time I allocated for 'television' in the evening to catch up.

IF ...	THEN...

Phoenix **JOURNAL**

> " The secret to making progress is to get started.
>
> Mark Twain "

Date:

....
....
....
....
....
....

Date:

....
....
....
....
....
....

JOURNAL

Date:

....
....
....
....
....
....
....
....

TOP TIP

Create 'happy reminders'. This could be putting a picture on the fridge or setting your phone to rotate your favourite pictures as your lock screen. You could even note them down and save them in a jar to read when you feel blue.

Date:

....
....
....
....
....
....
....
....

Date:

....
....
....
....
....
....
....
....

Affirmation

I am free to create the life I want.

I am free to...

Date:

....

....

....

....

....

....

....

Date:

....

....

....

....

....

....

WEEK 26: DISCIPLINE

'Discipline is choosing between what you want now and what you want most.'

This quote is often attributed to Abraham Lincoln, but whoever said it summed up perfectly the dilemma we are up against every day.

Below, list your 'want most's. Perhaps they include the ambitions that made you select The Phoenix Journal. Throughout the week, add items to your 'want now' column. At the end of the week, decide which are detrimental to your goal and cross them out. Even if you caved and indulged at the time, strike them out for future reference. How about those that may have impacted in a minor way on your goals? Underline them. They may be okay occasionally, but too often and they could become an obstacle. Review your sheet. Are you happy with the number of items crossed out or underlined?

WANT MOST	WANT NOW

Phoenix JOURNAL

> " Learn as if you will live forever, live like you will die tomorrow.
>
> Mahatma Gandhi "

Date:

....
....
....
....
....
....

Date:

....
....
....
....
....
....

Phoenix
JOURNAL

Making Connections

As a child, what was your dream job? Why?

Date:

....
....
....
....
....
....
....
....
....
....

Date:

....
....
....
....
....
....
....
....
....
....

Phoenix JOURNAL

Date:

....
....
....
....
....
....
....
....
....
....

TOP TIP

Listen to your body. Rest when you're tired, and stop eating when you're full; if it could, it would thank you for it.

Date:

....
....
....
....
....
....
....
....

Date:

....
....
....
....
....
....
....
....

WEEK 27: THE EFFORT SCALE 1

It may seem like the good things in life come easily to some. The truth is, it's very likely that they are just working harder than most. Focus on three people in your life who you believe are doing well. Look for evidence of the amount of effort they are putting in. This could include arriving early and staying late, volunteering for tasks, taking on roles of responsibility, turning down a treat that might have ruined a diet... the list is endless! On the thermometer below, write down any behaviours that reflect this level of effort underneath low, medium or high.

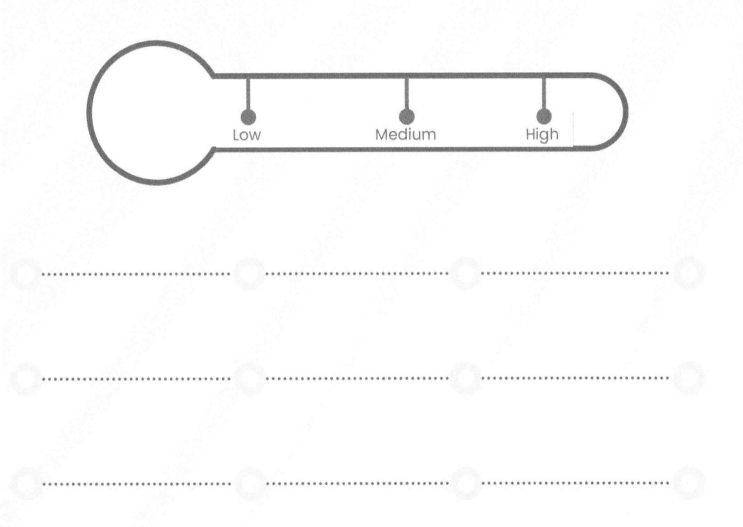

Low   Medium   High

JOURNAL

> "
> Life begins at the end of your comfort zone.
>
> Neale Donald Walsch
> "

Date:

....

....

....

....

....

....

Date:

....

....

....

....

....

....

JOURNAL

Date:

....
....
....
....
....
....
....
....
....
....

Affirmation

I choose to talk to
myself kindly.

I choose...

Date:

....
....
....
....
....
....
....
....

Date:

....
....
....
....
....
....
....
....

Phoenix
JOURNAL

Top Tip

When meeting someone for the first time, ask them what they like to do instead of what they do for a living. It will inspire a far better conversation.

Date:

....
....
....
....
....
....
....
....
....
....

Date:

....
....
....
....
....
....
....
....
....
....

WEEK 28: THE EFFORT SCALE 2

Repeat last week's activity, but use yourself as the subject. Don't limit yourself to work, but think about opportunities in your health, hobbies and relationships too.

Consider:
- What opportunities to put in effort have arisen?
- Where would you place yourself?

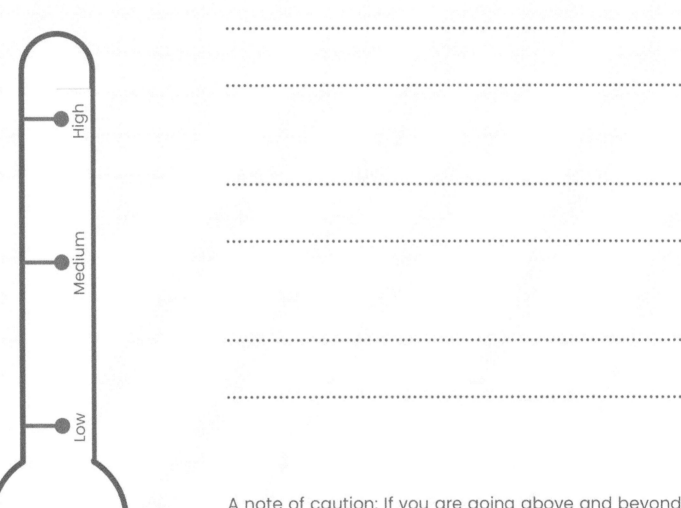

A note of caution: If you are going above and beyond professionally, ensure you are given credit for your work and your efforts are moving you towards a specific goal.

Phoenix
JOURNAL

Date:

....

....

....

....

....

....

Date:

....

....

....

....

....

....

Phoenix JOURNAL

Date:

....

....

....

....

....

....

....

....

....

Remember

Enjoy this moment because once it's gone, it's gone forever.

Date:

....

....

....

....

....

....

....

Date:

....

....

....

....

....

....

....

Phoenix JOURNAL

Making Connections

Do you have any phobias?

Date: _____

··
··
··
··
··
··
··
··
··
··
··

Date: _____

··
··
··
··
··
··
··
··
··
··
··

WEEK 29: THE EFFORT SCALE 3

Look at your scale from last week. Choose a situation where you did not put in maximum effort. Consider the questions below.

Would it have benefitted you to put in more effort? How?

....

....

....

What could you do differently this week?

....

....

....

Where would that move you to on the effort scale?

....

....

....

Phoenix
JOURNAL

> We learn from failure, not from success.
>
> Bram Stoker

Date:

....
....
....
....
....
....

Date:

....
....
....
....
....
....

Phoenix JOURNAL

Top Tip

Try not to compare yourself to others but, if you must, make the exercise productive. Is there anything you can learn from them?

Date:

Date:

JOURNAL

Date:

....

....

....

....

....

....

....

....

....

Affirmation

I am worthy of
love and affection.

I am worthy of...

Date:

....

....

....

....

....

....

....

....

Date:

....

....

....

....

....

....

....

....

WEEK 30: THE EARLY BIRD?

The early bird catches the worm.' Isn't that what they say? Well, some of us would like to catapult that early bird from our lives Angry Birds style. Buying into this myth can make us feel like a failure before even beginning our day. We are individuals, and our energy levels and schedules will reflect that. Additionally, there will be demands in our lives, such as children and work, affecting our energy levels. The key is to work with our bodies if possible.

Gain insight into how your energy levels vary by colour coding the timetable throughout the day. We will use this in a future activity to help you plan your day.

Sun	Mon	Tue	Wed	Thu	Fri	Sat

Black – Sleeping Green – Energised Amber – Neutral Red – Tired

Phoenix
JOURNAL

> The journey of a thousand miles begins with one step.
>
> Lao Tzu

Date:

....

....

....

....

....

....

Date:

....

....

....

....

....

....

Phoenix
JOURNAL

Making Connections

Which character in a book, television show or movie would you say was most like you? Why?

Date:

Date:

JOURNAL

Date:

....
....
....
....
....
....
....
....
....

Remember

Anger isn't a negative emotion, but you must learn to express it in a non-aggressive way.

Date:

....
....
....
....
....
....
....
....

Date:

....
....
....
....
....
....
....
....

WEEK 31: WHEEL OF LIFE

On a scale from 1 to 6 (with 6 being the ideal), how satisfied are you with each area of your life? Colour in the relevant number of sections. This will help you pinpoint the areas where you need to put the most effort.

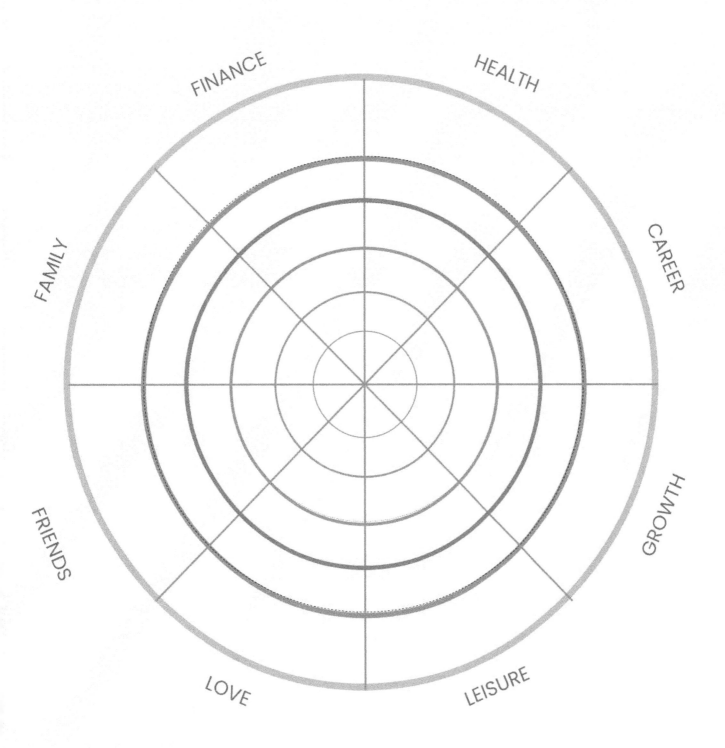

Phoenix
JOURNAL

> "
> Setting goals is the first step in turning the invisible into visible.
>
> Tony Robbins
> "

Date:

....

....

....

....

....

....

....

Date:

....

....

....

....

....

....

....

Phoenix JOURNAL

TOP TIP

Under promise and over deliver. Doing it the other way around sets you up for failure.

Date:

Date:

Date:

Affirmation

I can control my reactions to the behaviour of others.

I can control...

Date:

Date:

WEEK 32: WILL VERSUS SKILL

Whether a task feels insurmountable or is so dull that we can't face it, understanding our reactions can help us handle them better.

High skill/low will – Although accomplished at the task, you don't want to do it.
Low skill/low will – You aren't skilled in this area and aren't motivated to learn.
High skill/high will – You excel at tasks in this area and want to do them.
Low skill/high will – You aren't as confident at these tasks but want to learn.

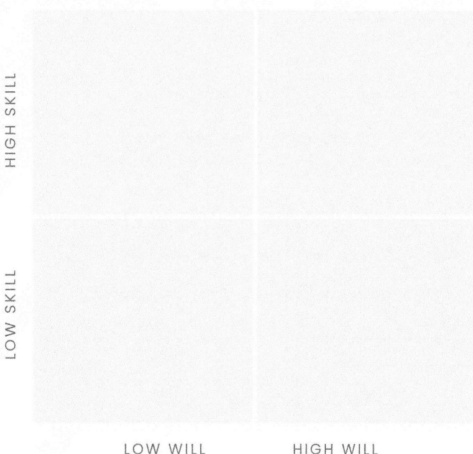

HIGH SKILL

LOW SKILL

LOW WILL   HIGH WILL

Reflect on the tasks ahead of you this week. Place them on the matrix above. For example: if you have been to the gym a thousand times but find it boring, that would be a high skill/low will task. However, if you are excited about your gym induction, that would be low skill/high will.

JOURNAL

> Be careful how you talk to
> yourself, because you are
> listening.
>
> Lisa Hayes

Date:

....
....
....
....
....
....

Date:

....
....
....
....
....
....

Phoenix JOURNAL

Date:

....

....

....

....

....

....

....

....

....

Remember

You are enough.

Date:

....

....

....

....

....

....

....

Date:

....

....

....

....

....

....

....

Phoenix
JOURNAL

Making Connections

What is your biggest regret?

Date: _____   Date: _____

....

....

....

....

....

....

....

....

....

....

WEEK 33: THREE SMALL STEPS

Look back at the last 'Three Small Steps' activity. Did you achieve your goal completely? Do you need to carry any tasks over to this activity? Write your new or revised goal in the space below and add the three steps you will take to complete it.

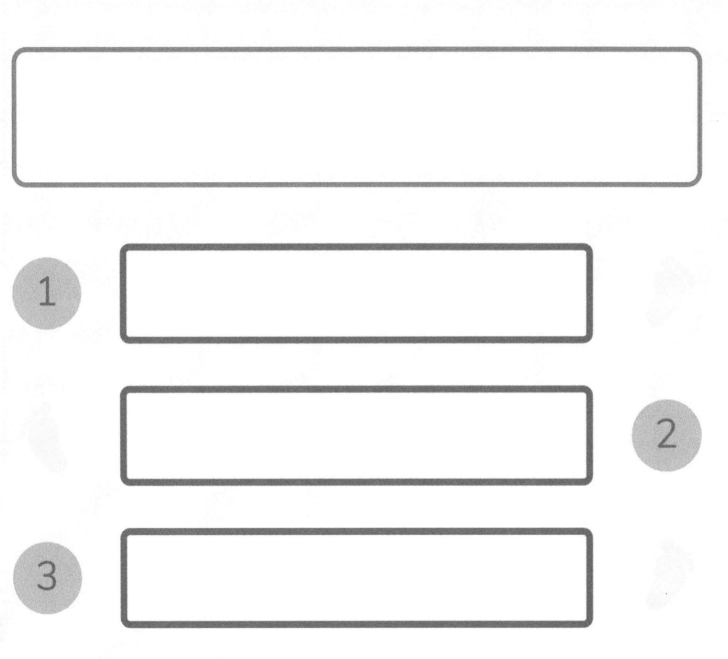

Phoenix JOURNAL

> " Genius is 1% inspiration, 99% perspiration.
>
> Thomas Edison
> "

Date:

....
....
....
....
....
....
....

Date:

....
....
....
....
....
....

Phoenix
JOURNAL

Top Tip

Choose experiences over materialistic objects. Memories last a lifetime.

Date:

....
....
....
....
....
....
....
....
....
....

Date:

....
....
....
....
....
....
....
....
....
....

Phoenix
JOURNAL

Date:

....
....
....
....
....
....
....
....
....
....

Remember

Don't confuse a bad day
with a bad life.

Date:

....
....
....
....
....
....
....
....
....
....
....

Date:

....
....
....
....
....
....
....
....
....
....
....

WEEK 34: PLOTTING THE JOURNEY

It is all very well being asked to plot the first three steps towards your goal. But what about all the ones that come after? If you aren't sure where you will go next, you need to do some research. Start with the questions below and then use your journal pages this week to add anything else you think of.

What questions do you have?

Where could you find the answers?

Which sites could you read up on?

Who can you ask?

How will you contact them?

Are there any deadlines you need to take note of?

JOURNAL

> **Experience is simply the name we give our mistakes.**
>
> Oscar Wilde

Date:

....

....

....

....

....

....

....

Date:

....

....

....

....

....

....

Phoenix
JOURNAL

Affirmation

My feelings are valid.

My feelings are...

Date:

....
....
....
....
....
....
....
....
....

Date:

....
....
....
....
....
....
....

Date:

....
....
....
....
....
....
....

Phoenix
JOURNAL

Making Connections

Do you have any role models?
What makes you admire them?

Date:

....
....
....
....
....
....
....
....
....
....

Date:

....
....
....
....
....
....
....
....
....
....

WEEK 35: A NEW DAY

Using your 'Will versus Skill' matrix, and 'Early Bird?' timetable, plan your schedule so that the low skill/low will tasks are when you feel most energised. Save the high skill/high will tasks for neutral or tired times of the day. Obviously, some tasks can't be timetabled as easily (e.g. parenting), but organising other tasks around them should allow your day to go more smoothly.

Sun	Mon	Tue	Wed	Thu	Fri	Sat

JOURNAL

> 66
>
> Success is a journey, not a destination.
>
> Arthur Ashe
>
> 99

Date:

....

....

....

....

....

....

Date:

....

....

....

....

....

....

Phoenix
JOURNAL

TOP TIP

If you find it difficult to say no,
then say not right now. People
tend to be impatient and if you
don't allow yourself to be the
immediate solution to their
problem, often they'll find
someone else.

Date:

Date:

Date:

Remember

Go into every day thinking about what you can add to the world, not what you can take from it.

Date: | Date:

································ ································
································ ································
································ ································
································ ································
································ ································
································ ································
································ ································
································ ································
································ ································
································ ································
································ ································
································ ································

WEEK 36: HOW RESILIENT?

Resilience is a crucial feature of successful people. Think about the most successful people that you know. How do they react to obstacles? Look at the resilience criteria below and decide how much you agree with each one, 1 being the least and 5 the most.

	1	2	3	4	5
I always finish what I begin.					
I am happy to receive feedback, even if it is negative.					
When I fail, I consider what I can learn from it.					
I focus on one project at a time.					
I seek advice from more knowledgeable others.					
I volunteer for tasks outside my comfort zone.					
I answer questions even if I'm not sure I'm correct.					
I enjoy learning new skills.					

Which area will you try to improve?	
When have you been most resilient?	
How might you apply more resilience to a present task?	

Phoenix JOURNAL

> Whether you think you can, or you think you can't – you're right.
>
> Henry Ford

Date:

....

....

....

....

....

....

Date:

....

....

....

....

....

....

Phoenix
JOURNAL

Affirmation

I surround myself with people who support and motivate me.

I surround myself with...

....
....
....
....
....
....
....
....
....

Date:

....
....
....
....
....
....
....

Date:

....
....
....
....
....
....
....

Phoenix JOURNAL

Making Connections

What is your biggest fear?

Date:

....
....
....
....
....
....
....
....
....
....
....

Date:

....
....
....
....
....
....
....
....
....
....
....

WEEK 37: UPON REFLECTION

Obstacles and setbacks may seem unfair or annoying. Perhaps the impact went further than this and turned your life onto a completely different course. At the time, it may seem that taking anything positive from these events is impossible. But on reflection, we may find they have influenced us positively in ways we didn't anticipate. For example: a chronic illness that brings us closer to friends and family; a job loss that gives us the courage to begin a new career. But as nobody else has experienced it from your point of view, only you can find it. Think back to a difficult situation you have faced. Consider the following prompt questions:

Have you developed a personal quality or skill due to what you faced?

Did you review life goals or priorities?

Do you appreciate any aspects of your life more as a result?

Have any of your relationships been strengthened as a result of your obstacle?

Even if the questions above didn't resonate with you, whilst journaling this week, look for any positives that result from the challenges you face.

JOURNAL

> Education is the most powerful weapon which you can use to change the world.
>
> Nelson Mandela

Date:

....
....
....
....
....
....

Date:

....
....
....
....
....
....

Phoenix JOURNAL

Remember

Time is the most precious thing you have. Spend it wisely.

Date:

....
....
....
....
....
....
....
....

Date:

....
....
....
....
....
....
....

Date:

....
....
....
....
....
....
....

Affirmation

I choose to celebrate my efforts and welcome mistakes as learning opportunities.

I choose to...

Date:

....
....
....
....
....
....

Date:

....
....
....
....
....
....

WEEK 38: OBSTACLES

Below, list as many obstacles to achieving your goal as you can. For example: money, lack of time, health, family commitments, professional qualifications, work experience, location... The list is as limitless as the goals that accompany them.

Now place the obstacles somewhere in the circles below. The inner circle is where you will place things over which you have complete control, the next circle means some control, and the outer circle means no control. This week take note of potential obstacles and add them to your circles.

OBSTACLE LIST

Phoenix JOURNAL

> It is better to fail in originality than to succeed in imitation.
>
> Herman Melville

Date:

....

....

....

....

....

....

Date:

....

....

....

....

....

....

....

Phoenix JOURNAL

Affirmation

My life is full of happiness.

My life is full of...

Date:

....
....
....
....
....
....
....
....
....

Date:

....
....
....
....
....
....
....
....
....

Date:

....
....
....
....
....
....
....
....
....

Phoenix JOURNAL

Making Connections

What would you consider your guilty pleasure?

Date:

Date:

....
....
....
....
....
....
....
....
....
....
....

WEEK 39: MOVING THE BOULDER

This activity will take a little trust. Choose somebody with whom you are comfortable sharing the items you placed in the 'no control' circle. Ask them if they can see any possible strategies to move the obstacles into the 'some control' area. Sometimes we need a fresh perspective to begin moving that metaphorical boulder. Consider the following questions:

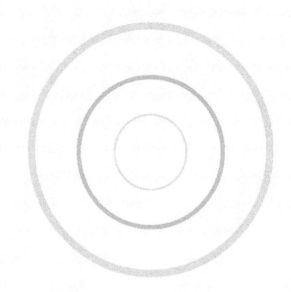

Are any of your obstacles moveable?

What steps could you take to achieve this?

Will you need any help? From whom and what will you ask of them?

Will you need any other resources? What are they and where will you get them?

Phoenix
JOURNAL

> " A person who never made a mistake never tried anything new.
>
> Albert Einstein "

Date:

....
....
....
....
....
....

Date:

....
....
....
....
....
....

Phoenix
JOURNAL

Date:

Date:

JOURNAL

Date:

....
....
....
....
....
....
....
....
....

TOP TIP

There is a theory that you are the average of the five people that you surround yourself with most. Ask yourself whether their characteristics are the ones you want for yourself.

Date:

....
....
....
....
....
....
....
....

Date:

....
....
....
....
....
....
....
....

WEEK 40: THE ENEMY OF DONE

'Perfect' is the enemy of done. It is undefined. Unachievable. You might fly past every deadline set and still not achieve perfection. 'Excellent', however, is the best that you can do. It allows for mistakes and learning opportunities. You can define it with tangible features. You can explain why it is as good as you believe whilst allowing for an 'even better if'. Depending on the task, 'good enough' might be an acceptable point at which you can say the task is complete. If putting any more time or resources into the goal won't add significant value to the outcome, then why bother? Consider the following questions:

Does the outcome need to be 'excellent' or just 'good enough'?

What will that look like?

What is the deadline to achieve this goal?

Phoenix
JOURNAL

> " I never dreamed about success. I worked for it.
>
> Estée Lauder "

Date:

....

....

....

....

....

....

Date:

....

....

....

....

....

....

Phoenix JOURNAL

Date:

Affirmation

Every day I take a step closer toward fulfilling my goals.

Everyday I take a step closer toward...

Date:

Date:

Phoenix JOURNAL

Making Connections

What three words best describe you?

Date:

....

....

....

....

....

....

....

....

....

....

Date:

....

....

....

....

....

....

....

....

....

....

WEEK 41: IN THEIR FOOTSTEPS

You probably are not the first to go on this journey. Others have likely accomplished what you have set out to do. You can look for the clues they have left behind and use them as a trail to follow.

Pick somebody you can use as a role model. Think about the steps they must have taken. Look for clues as to what these were. If it's somebody in the public eye, you may wish to read or watch interviews they have done.

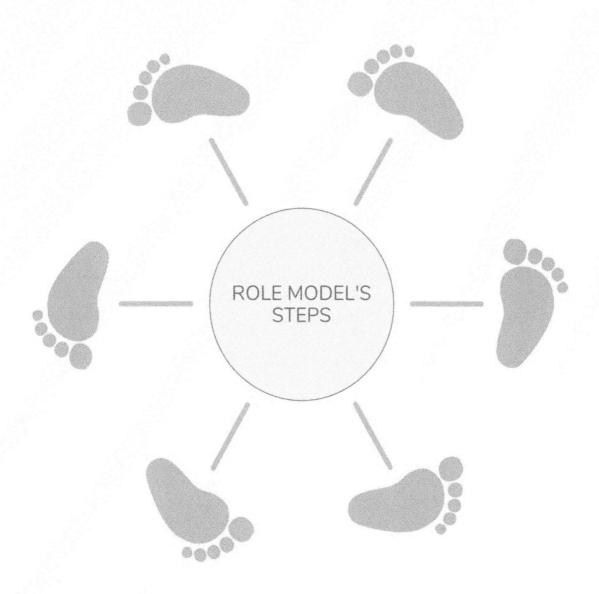

Phoenix
JOURNAL

Date:

....

....

....

....

....

....

Date:

....

....

....

....

....

....

JOURNAL

Date:

Date:

Date:

Affirmation

Every day I strive to be the best version of myself.

Every day I strive to...

Date:

....
....
....
....
....
....

Date:

....
....
....
....
....
....
....

WEEK 42: IN THEIR FOOTSTEPS 2

Imagine you are your role model and answer the following questions as if you are that person. If it is somebody you know in real life, you could ask them.

What was your dream or aspiration? What made you select it?

What obstacles did you encounter in achieving your dream?

Was there a time you received negative or constructive feedback? What was your reaction?

What advice would you give to somebody just setting out on the path you chose?

JOURNAL

> 66
>
> Don't let yesterday take up too much of today.
>
> Will Rogers
>
> 99

Date:

....
....
....
....
....
....
....

Date:

....
....
....
....
....
....
....

Phoenix
JOURNAL

Making Connections

Where is your dream holiday destination?
Why?

Date:

Date:

JOURNAL

Date:

Remember

The majority of the people in the world don't think about you at all. In a way, that removes the pressure for you to care about everyone else. Focus on yourself first and then on the people who have earned your time and consideration.

Date:

Date:

WEEK 43: THREE CS

This week, list the concerns that pop into your head. Review each one and decide if you have any control over the outcome. For example: if you are about to have a job interview, you have no control over whether a more qualified candidate applies. This would go under concern. It's best to try and put these items out of your head. However, the 'questions that the interviewer might ask' is an area that you could move over to the control column. In the counteract column, list actions you can take to make yourself feel less anxious. For example: researching common interview questions for that field, practising with a friend, etc.

CONCERN	CONTROL	COUNTERACT

Phoenix
JOURNAL

> "
> The pessimist sees difficulty in every opportunity. The optimist sees opportunity in every difficulty.
>
> Winston Churchill
> "

Date:

....
....
....
....
....
....

Date:

....
....
....
....
....
....

JOURNAL

Date:

·······································
·······································
·······································
·······································
·······································
·······································
·······································
·······································

TOP TIP

Stop telling yourself that your negative emotions shouldn't exist. Instead, think about what they are telling you. If you need or want to make a change, then make a plan to do so.

Date:

·······································
·······································
·······································
·······································
·······································
·······································
·······································
·······································

Date:

·······································
·······································
·······································
·······································
·······································
·······································
·······································
·······································

Phoenix
JOURNAL

Making Connections

What is your most annoying habit?
What habit do you find most annoying in others?

Date:

Date:

WEEK 44: OUT OF THE TORNADO

Sometimes our worries can feel like a tornado, gathering us from the safety of our lives. The invasive thoughts rumbling through our heads just won't give up the hold they have on us. In this situation we are completely fixated, perhaps justifiably so, on ourselves.

How do we escape? A simple activity that can have amazing effects can be shifting our attention from our own concerns to the happiness of others. Choose three people in your life that you care for. Spend just a minute or two listing the hopes and wishes you have for them. You may find that diverting your focus in this positive way breaks the negative cycle.

1.........

2.........

3.........

Phoenix JOURNAL

> Nothing in the world can take the place of persistence. Talent will not; nothing is more common than unsuccessful men with talent.
>
> Calvin Coolidge

Date:

....

....

....

....

....

....

Date:

....

....

....

....

....

....

....

Phoenix JOURNAL

Date:

....
....
....
....
....
....
....
....
....
....

Affirmation

I have the power to create change in my life.

I have the power to...

Date:

....
....
....
....
....
....
....

Date:

....
....
....
....
....
....
....

Phoenix JOURNAL

Date:

....

....

....

....

....

....

....

....

....

....

....

Date:

....

....

....

....

....

....

....

....

....

....

....

WEEK 45: GAINING PERSPECTIVE

Another method of quieting our brains is to gain some perspective on our problems. Will it affect you in five years? If not, don't waste more than five minutes fretting about it. However, sometimes that is easier said than done, so here is another method to try.

Start by describing your worry in the 'Before' section below. Then do something that makes you feel small. Go for a walk in the woods, stare at the night sky, or throw pebbles into the sea. In the 'After' section, describe how you are feeling now. You may find that what you were fretting over doesn't matter that much after all.

BEFORE

AFTER

Phoenix JOURNAL

> " Develop success from failures. Discouragement and failure are two of the surest stepping stones to success.
>
> Dale Carnegie "

Date:

....
....
....
....
....
....

Date:

....
....
....
....
....
....

Phoenix
JOURNAL

Making Connections

Have you ever saved a life?

Date:

Date:

Phoenix JOURNAL

Date:

....
....
....
....
....
....
....
....
....

Remember

Embrace change.
It's how you grow.

Date:

....
....
....
....
....
....
....
....

Date:

....
....
....
....
....
....
....
....

WEEK 46: THE THIEF OF TIME

'Procrastination is the thief of time.'
Edward Young said that back in the 17th century. Human nature doesn't change, and I'm sure most of us are still guilty of this flaw. Sometimes a decision or task seems so immense that we put it off. Or perhaps it is just mundane. Either way, our lack of action can lead to anxiety and likely further procrastination.

To gain some insight, think about the last task you procrastinated on and consider the following questions:

What was the task?

What made the task so unappealing to you?

Were there any negative consequences of your procrastination?

Phoenix JOURNAL

> " Our lives improve only when we take chances - and the first and most difficult risk we can take is to be honest with ourselves.
>
> Walter Anderson "

Date:

....

....

....

....

....

....

Date:

....

....

....

....

....

....

Phoenix JOURNAL

Date:

....

....

....

....

....

....

....

....

TOP TIP

Embrace uncertainty. That uncomfortable feeling you get when you don't have all the answers is due to personal growth. Don't dismiss or avoid it.

Date:

....

....

....

....

....

....

....

Date:

....

....

....

....

....

....

....

Affirmation

I treat myself as I would a dear friend.

I treat myself...

Date:

....
....
....
....
....
....
....

Date:

....
....
....
....
....
....
....

WEEK 47: PROCRASTINATION

Break the procrastination habit! Consider a task you have been procrastinating on recently and make a plan to overcome it. This should alleviate some anxiety and free you to focus on other goals. These questions will help you formulate your strategy.

What is the task?

....

Why is it important?

....

When will you achieve it by?

....

Do you need help achieving it?

....

If so, who could you ask?

....

TASK

PLAN

JOURNAL

> When you give joy to other people, you get more joy in return. You should give a good thought to the happiness that you can give out.
>
> Eleanor Roosevelt

Date:

....

....

....

....

....

....

Date:

....

....

....

....

....

....

JOURNAL

Remember

Focus on the present because you can't change the past.

Date:

Date:

Phoenix JOURNAL

Making Connections

Who influenced the person you are today the most?
Was their effect positive or negative?

Date:

....

....

....

....

....

....

....

....

....

....

Date:

....

....

....

....

....

....

....

....

....

....

WEEK 48: WHEEL OF LIFE

On a scale from 1 to 6 (with 6 being the ideal), how satisfied are you with each area of your life? Colour in the relevant number of sections. This will help you pinpoint the areas where you need to put the most effort.

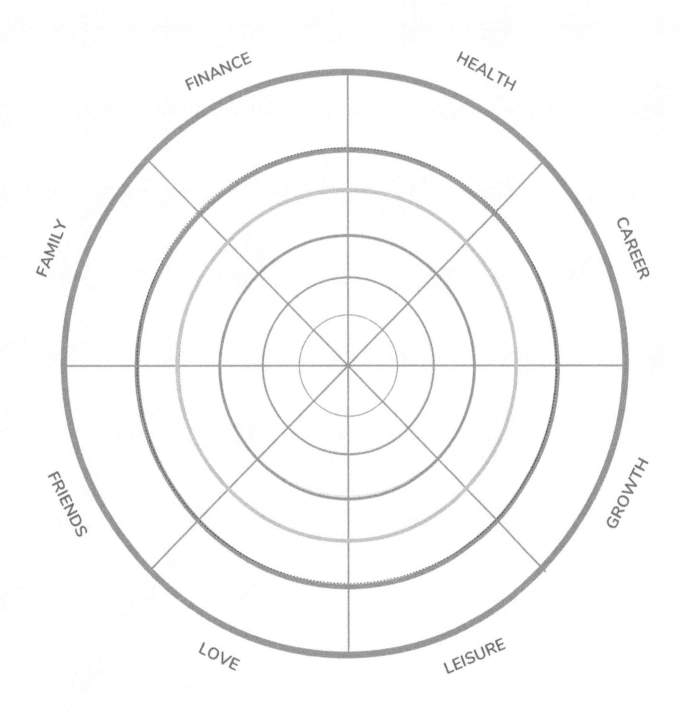

JOURNAL

> 66
>
> Stay away from those people who try to disparage your ambitions. Small minds will always do that, but great minds will give you a feeling that you can become great too.
>
> Mark Twain
>
> 99

Date:

....

....

....

....

....

....

....

Date:

....

....

....

....

....

....

....

Phoenix
JOURNAL

Remember

Share your emotions with friends and family. It helps build
connections and understanding.

Date:

Date:

JOURNAL

Date:

Affirmation

I give myself permission to rest and recharge so I am the healthiest version of myself.

I give myself permission to...

Date:

Date:

WEEK 49: EMOTIONAL VAMPIRES

It may be hard to hear, but your friends may not be good for you. List the three friends closest to you. Now consider how you feel after spending some time with them. Can you pinpoint why?

For example:

Amy — I feel drained because she vents and complains the whole time.

Caleb — I feel energised because he is always so optimistic.

If you have friends like Amy, you may be dealing with an emotional vampire, someone who (perhaps unconsciously) drains you or your energy and your drive. You may baulk at spending less time with them, but you should at least be aware of their influence and the potential obstacles they might present in reaching your goals.

1.

2.

3.

JOURNAL

> Experience is a hard teacher because she gives the test first, and the lesson afterwards.
>
> Vernon Sanders Law

Date:

....

....

....

....

....

....

Date:

....

....

....

....

....

....

Phoenix JOURNAL

Making Connections

When you're in a bad mood, how do you improve it?

Date:

....
....
....
....
....
....
....
....
....
....

Date:

....
....
....
....
....
....
....
....
....
....

JOURNAL

Date:

....
....
....
....
....
....
....
....
....

TOP TIP

Focus on one goal at a time. Nobody is saying you can't have it all, but it might not be achievable all at once.

Date:

....
....
....
....
....
....
....

Date:

....
....
....
....
....
....
....

WEEK 50: THE ROTTEN APPLE

One rotten apple can spoil the whole barrel. It's the same when we have destructive or problematic people in our lives. Of course, a huge part of self-development is accountability and owning our mistakes. However, it is also essential to reflect on any negative influences that might be pushing us toward bad decisions. This could be people we are spending time with or places we go. Once we recognise any negativity, we can decide what we can do to change it. Think back to a poor decision and consider the following questions.

Where and when did it happen?

....

....

How were you feeling?

....

....

Did you consciously make the poor decision or did a series of events lead to it?

....

....

Did you make the decision alone or were others involved?

....

....

Was your decision detrimental to anybody's well-being besides your own?

....

....

JOURNAL

> I'm a greater believer in luck, and I find the harder I work the more I have of it.
>
> Thomas Jefferson

Date:

....

....

....

....

....

....

Date:

....

....

....

....

....

....

Phoenix
JOURNAL

Date:

> **Remember**
>
> Forgiveness sets you free.
> Don't let anyone live rent
> free in your head.

Date:

Date:

Affirmation

I feel proud of the progress I have made towards my goals.

I feel proud of...

Date:

....
....
....
....
....
....

Date:

....
....
....
....
....
....

WEEK 51: THREE SMALL STEPS

Look back at the last 'Three Small Steps' activity. Did you achieve your goal completely? Do you need to carry any tasks over to this activity? Write your new or revised goal in the space below and add the three steps you will take to complete it.

1

2

3

JOURNAL

> The most difficult thing is the decision to act, the rest is merely tenacity.
>
> Amelia Earhart

Date:

....
....
....
....
....
....

Date:

....
....
....
....
....
....

Phoenix
JOURNAL

Making Connections

What historical character would you invite to a dinner party? What would you ask them?

Date:

....
....
....
....
....
....
....
....
....
....
....

Date:

....
....
....
....
....
....
....
....
....
....
....

Phoenix
JOURNAL

Date:

....
....
....
....
....
....
....
....
....

Remember

Nobody ever said on their deathbed, 'I wish I'd worked more. Goals and ambitions are important, but remember, you're replaceable at work, not at home. Keep a work/life balance.

Date:

....
....
....
....
....
....
....
....

Date:

....
....
....
....
....
....
....
....

WEEK 52: PLOTTING THE JOURNEY

It is all very well being asked to plot the first three steps towards your goal. But what about all of the ones that come after? If you aren't sure where you will go next, you need to do some research. Start with the questions below and then use your journal pages this week to add anything else you think of.

What questions do you have?

Where could you find the answers?

Which sites could you read up on?

Who can you ask?

How will you contact them?

Are there any deadlines you need to take note of?

Phoenix
JOURNAL

> And the day came when the risk to remain tight in a bud was more painful than the risk it took to blossom.
>
> Anaïs Nin

Date:

....
....
....
....
....
....

Date:

....
....
....
....
....
....

JOURNAL

Date:

....

....

....

....

....

....

....

....

....

Affirmation

I am making space in my life for relaxation by maintaining a work/life balance.

I am making space in my life for...

Date:

....

....

....

....

....

....

....

....

Date:

....

....

....

....

....

....

....

....

Phoenix
JOURNAL

Making Connections

Where do you see yourself in a year? How about in a decade?

Date:

Date:

ABOUT THE AUTHOR

The activities within *The Phoenix Journal* were developed throughout a decade of leading schools on aspirational and growth mindset thinking both in the U.K. and the Middle East. After years of training educators, I decided to spread my message further by documenting some of the activities within *The Phoenix Journal*.

These ideals are also expressed through my series of children's rhyming picture books, which are published under the name Cher Louise Jones. When not writing for children, I create foreboding dystopian visions of the future for adults. Mixing the riveting but bleak with the quirky and upbeat brings a healthy balance to my writing life. My dystopian books include *Spiral Fracture, Jump* and the Escaping Sanctuary series.

On a more personal note, as a cancer survivor, I feel I have faced greater obstacles than most. Of course, the fact I'm still here is down to a mixture of reasons, from the amazing NHS to my incredible friends and family. But I also credit goal setting. I wasn't going to die without releasing my stories into the world. I accomplished that, so I set myself another goal, and another. I'm far too busy to give up fighting. Yes, I genuinely am that stubborn.

I hope you enjoyed the activities within *The Phoenix Journal*. It seemed only fitting to end on 'Plotting the Journey' because it doesn't end here. You need to take the skills you have learned and keep moving forward. I know these activities work because I use them. Now I want to share them with you. Because at some point we are all tested. It is our prerogative to wallow in our misery. Or we can choose to be the phoenix and rise above it.

FOR FURTHER INFORMATION ABOUT MY WORK VISIT
CHERJONES.CO.UK

Ingram Content Group UK Ltd.
Milton Keynes UK
UKHW050639120623
423291UK00011B/429